WHOSE EYES ARE THESE?

JOANNE RANDOLPH

PowerKiDS
press.

New York

Published in 2009 by The Rosen Publishing Group, Inc.
29 East 21st Street, New York, NY 10010

First Edition

Book Design: Julio Gil
Photo Researcher: Jessica Gerweck

Photo Credits: Cover © Arte Wolfe/Getty Images; pp. 5, 7, 9, 11, 13, 15, 17, 19, 21, 23, 24 (top left, top right, bottom) Shutterstock.com.

Library of Congress Cataloging-in-Publication Data

Randolph, Joanne.
  Whose eyes are these? / Joanne Randolph. — 1st ed.
      p. cm. — (Animal clues)
  Includes index.
  ISBN 978-1-4042-4453-5 (library binding)
  1. Eye—Juvenile literature. I. Title.
  QL949.R27 2009
  590—dc22
                                                        2007048202

Manufactured in the United States of America

CONTENTS

Whose sharp, orange eyes help it hunt?

This owl's sharp, orange eyes help it hunt.

Whose green eyes are really made up of lots of small eyes?

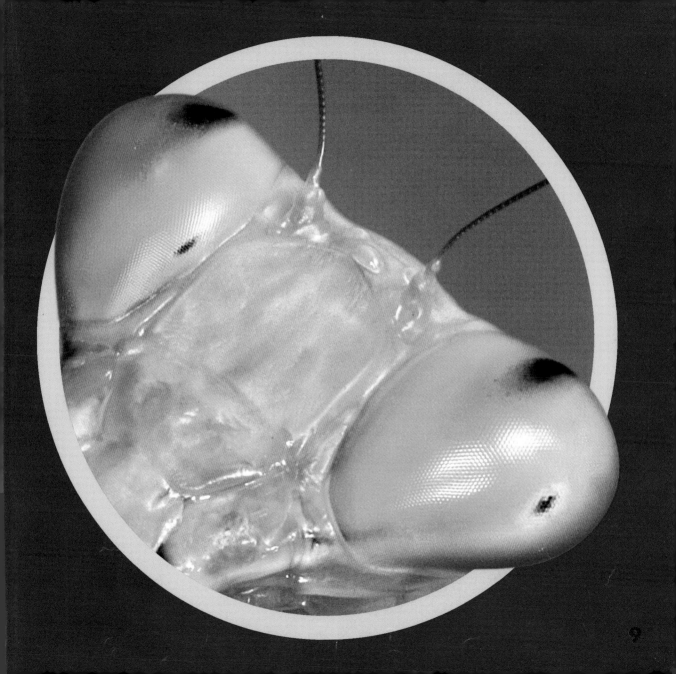

A praying mantis has green eyes made up of lots of small eyes.

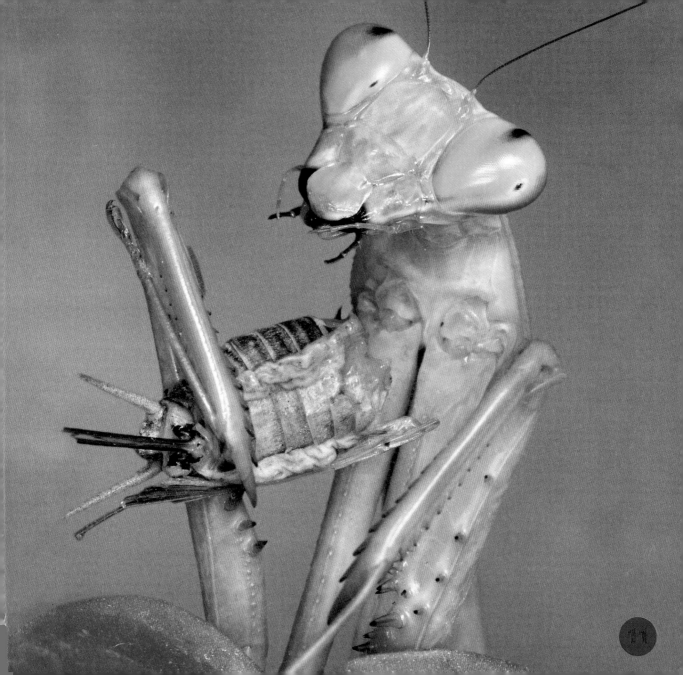

Which big cat's eyes are set in a **striped** face?

A tiger's eyes are set in a striped face.

Whose eyes have colorful **scales** all around them?

A chameleon's eyes have colorful scales all around them.

Whose eyes are these, sitting on top of **stems**?

This crab's eyes are sitting on top of stems.

WORDS TO KNOW

scales

stems

striped

INDEX

WEB SITES

Due to the changing nature of Internet links, PowerKids Press has developed an online list of Web sites related to the subject of this book. This site is updated regularly. Please use this link to access the list:
www.powerkidslinks.com/acl/eyes/